The Day the Earth Stood Still

Chicago, Illinois

© 2006 Raintree
Published by Raintree,
A division of Reed Elsevier, Inc.
Chicago, Illinois

Customer Service   888–363–4266

Visit our website at www.heinemannraintree.com

Printed and bound in the United States by Lake Book
Manufacturing, Inc.

10 09 08 07 06
10 9 8 7 6 5 4 3 2 1

**Library of Congress Cataloging-in-
Publication Data**
Thomas, Isabel, 1980-
  The day the Earth stood still : Earth's movement in
space / Isabel
Thomas.
    p. cm. -- (Fusion)
  Includes bibliographical references and index.
  ISBN 1-4109-1930-7 (library binding-hardcover) --
ISBN 1-4109-1961-7
(pbk.)
  1. Earth--Rotation--Juvenile literature. 2. Earth--
Orbit--Juvenile
literature. 3. Seasons--Juvenile literature. I. Title. II.
Fusion
(Chicago, Ill.)
  QB633.T56 2006
  523'.35--dc22
                                    2005016486

Acknowledgments
The author and publishers are grateful to the
following for permission to reproduce copyright
material: Alamy p. 23 (Andre Jenny); Digital Vision
p. 21; FLPA/FotoNatura/Dietmar Nil pp. 8–9; Getty
Images/Photodisc pp. 6–7, 13, 21; Harcourt Education
Ltd. pp. 18–19 (Jeff Edwards), 20 (Peter Evans);
Holt Studios p. 10; iStockPhoto p. 21 (Frank Pathol);
Photolibrary.com p. 24 (Owen Newman); Science
Photo Library pp. 17, 27, 19 (Dr. Juerg Alean,
www.stromboli.net), 18 (Martin Riedl),
5 (M-SAT Ltd.), 15 (Pekka Parviainen).

Cover photograph of Earth from space, reproduced
with permission of Science Photo Library
(David Nunuk).

Illustrations by Darren Lingard.

The publishers would like to thank Nancy Harris
for her assistance in the preparation of this book.

Every effort has been made to contact copyright
holders of any material reproduced in this book.
Any omissions will be rectified in subsequent
printings if notice is given to the publishers.

The paper used to print this book comes from
sustainable resources.

Contents

Some words are printed in bold, **like this**. You can find out what they mean on page 30. You can also look in the box at the bottom of the page where they first appear.

Spinning Through Space

We don't feel like we are spinning when we stand on Earth. But, in fact, Earth is moving very fast. The ground at the **equator** is spinning at 1,000 miles (1,600 kilometers) per hour! The equator is an imaginary line. It is around the middle of Earth.

Earth spins (**rotates**) around an imaginary line. The line runs through its center. This line is called Earth's **axis**. It takes 24 hours (one day) for Earth to turn once on its axis.

Earth also moves around the Sun. The path that Earth takes around the Sun is called an **orbit**. It takes about 365 days (one year) for Earth to orbit once around the Sun.

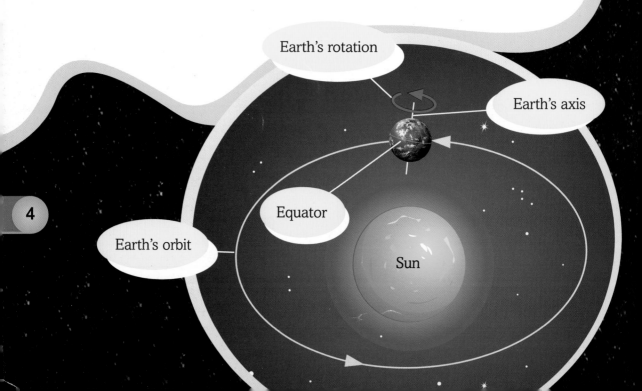

Earth's rotation

Earth's axis

Equator

Earth's orbit

Sun

▼ *Every year Earth takes us 590 million miles (950 million kilometers) around the Sun!*

axis	imaginary line passing through the center of Earth
equator	imaginary line around the middle of Earth
orbit	move around something on a fixed path
rotate	spin or turn on an axis

Which Side Are You On?

The place where you live is always moving. This is because Earth is always **rotating** (spinning) on its **axis**. It moves in and out of the Sun's light. This gives us night and day.

What if Earth stopped spinning on its **axis**, but continued to **orbit** the Sun? This could never happen. Yet think how life would change if it did happen!

There would be no sunrise and sunset every 24 hours. Instead, the place where you live would have sunlight for one half of the year. Then, you would be in darkness the other half of the year. You would be in darkness for six whole months!

Day and night

The half of Earth that is facing the Sun is lit up by sunlight. The other half is in shadow. When the place where you live is facing the Sun, it is daytime. As Earth moves, your home moves into darkness. It is nighttime.

Directio

Sleepless

If Earth stood still, things would change outside.
The place where you live would have daylight for half
a year. Then, it would have darkness for half a year. This
would be a disaster for life on Earth. Living things need
a pattern of daylight and darkness every 24 hours.

▼ Many animals live by patterns
of night and day. Bats hunt
for their food at night.

Most living things change their behavior from day to night. When it gets dark, humans feel tired. We know that it is time to sleep. If we had daylight for six months, our bodies would not know when to sleep. Many birds and animals would not know when to sleep, either.

Sleeping would not be the only problem. **Nocturnal** animals hunt for their food at night. They would become hungry and confused in endless daylight. Animals that could not change their behavior would die.

Where did the food go?

Plants also need patterns of light and darkness. Constant sunlight for six months might be too hot and bright for most plants. Darkness for six months would be even worse.

Green plants need light to make sugary food in their leaves. They use the food to grow. The way that plants make food in their leaves is called **photosynthesis**. Photosynthesis uses **energy** from sunlight to make food. It cannot happen in the dark. Plants in darkness would die very quickly.

Animals and humans need plants for food. We get energy to live and grow from eating plants. We also eat the meat of plant-eating animals. This is called the **food chain**.

If you put a plant in a ▶ dark cupboard, it would die very quickly.

energy	ability to cause a change or make something move
food chain	way animals are linked to other animals and to plants by what they eat
photosynthesis	how green plants make sugary food using light energy

A food chain

▼ The arrows show how energy passes through a food chain.

Plants make food using light from the Sun.

Animals, such as bears and humans, eat both plants and other animals.

Plant-eating animals eat plants.

Meat-eating animals eat other animals.

Extreme Weather

The Sun gives us heat **energy** as well as light energy. As Earth spins, energy from the Sun warms the air and ground during the day. At night the air and ground cool down. This pattern helps to make the temperature on Earth just right for animals and plants.

If Earth stopped spinning, the side facing the Sun would get hotter and hotter. On the dark side, it would quickly become freezing cold. Lakes, rivers, and parts of the ocean would turn to ice. Hot or cold, life would become difficult.

Winds are caused by air rushing from a hotter place to a colder place. Imagine how strong the winds would be if part of the world was freezing cold and part was boiling hot!

Hot fact!

The hottest recorded temperature on Earth was 134 °F (56.7 °C), in Death Valley, California. It got that hot during just one day. Imagine how hot Earth would be after months of endless sunlight!

hurricane   tropical storm with very fast winds

▼ **Hurricanes** form over warm seawater. If Earth stopped spinning, every ocean would face the Sun for months at a time. The water would heat up so much that the storms would be enormous.

The magnetosphere

Deep under the surface of Earth, there is a layer of hot, liquid metal. As Earth spins, this metal swirls around. The swirling liquid metal produces a **magnetic field**. The magnetic field is called the magnetosphere.

The magnetosphere protects Earth from dangerous rays from the Sun. If Earth stopped spinning (**rotating**), the magnetic field would disappear. The Sun's dangerous rays would reach Earth. To survive, we would need to live in special buildings. We would need to wear space suits like astronauts.

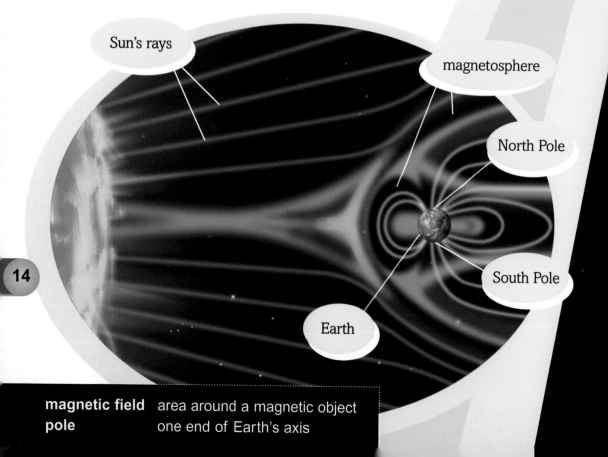

Sun's rays

magnetosphere

North Pole

South Pole

Earth

magnetic field	area around a magnetic object
pole	one end of Earth's axis

▼Earth's rotation helps to block dangerous rays from space. Some of these rays can get through Earth's magnetic field at the North and South **poles**. They make the air glow in many colors.

15

A light in the sky

Earth is not the only thing that moves in an **orbit**. The Moon orbits around Earth.

The Moon does not make its own light. It shines in the night sky because it is lit up by the Sun. Each night we see a different part of the sunlit side of the Moon. The different shapes that we see are called **phases** of the Moon.

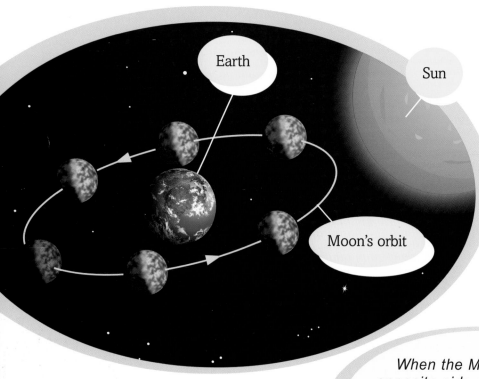

Earth

Sun

Moon's orbit

When the Moon is on the ▶ opposite side of Earth from the Sun, we can see the whole of its sunlit side. This is called a full moon.

force	something that acts to change the movement or shape of an object
gravity	force that pulls large objects toward each other
phases	stages

Gravity is a **force** that pulls large objects toward each other. As Earth spins, the pull of the Moon's gravity makes the oceans rise and fall. This is called high tide and low tide. High tide happens twice a day. If Earth stopped **rotating**, high tide would only happen twice a month. Sea animals and plants that depend on the tides would die.

17

Earth will never ▼ stop rotating, but it is slowing down!

friction   force that slows two objects down if they are touching each other

Slowing down!

When something is spinning, it will keep spinning until a **force** slows it down. A spinning basketball slows down because of **friction** between the ball and the finger. Something like this is happening to Earth.

There is a bit of friction between the tides and the spinning Earth. This is causing Earth's spin (**rotation**) to slow down a little each year. However, it will take millions of years before humans would notice a change!

When you are standing ▼ on Earth, it looks like the Sun is moving across the sky. Yet it is not the Sun that moves. It is Earth!

19

Twisting and Turning

The **equator** divides Earth into two halves. These halves are called the Northern **Hemisphere** and the Southern Hemisphere. Earth always tilts in the same direction on its **axis** as it travels around the Sun. So, when one hemisphere is tilted toward the Sun, the other hemisphere is tilted away from the Sun.

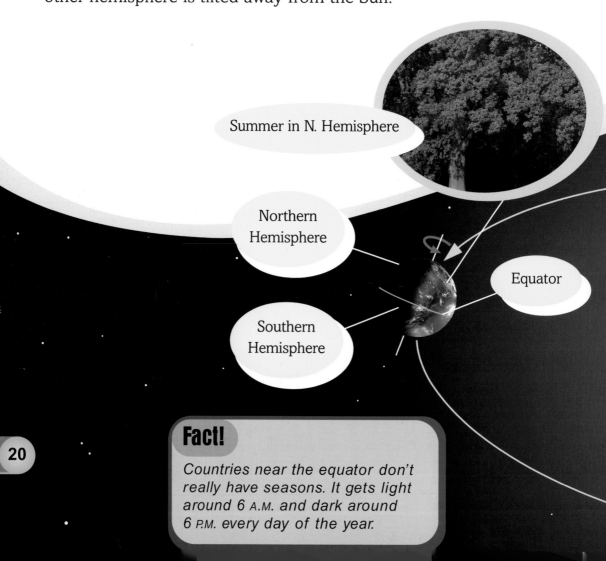

Summer in N. Hemisphere

Northern Hemisphere

Equator

Southern Hemisphere

Fact!

Countries near the equator don't really have seasons. It gets light around 6 A.M. and dark around 6 P.M. every day of the year.

When the Northern Hemisphere is tilted away from the Sun, it is winter. When it is tilted toward the Sun, it is summer. Earth is not tilted toward or away from the Sun in spring and fall. Both hemispheres get almost the same amount of sunlight.

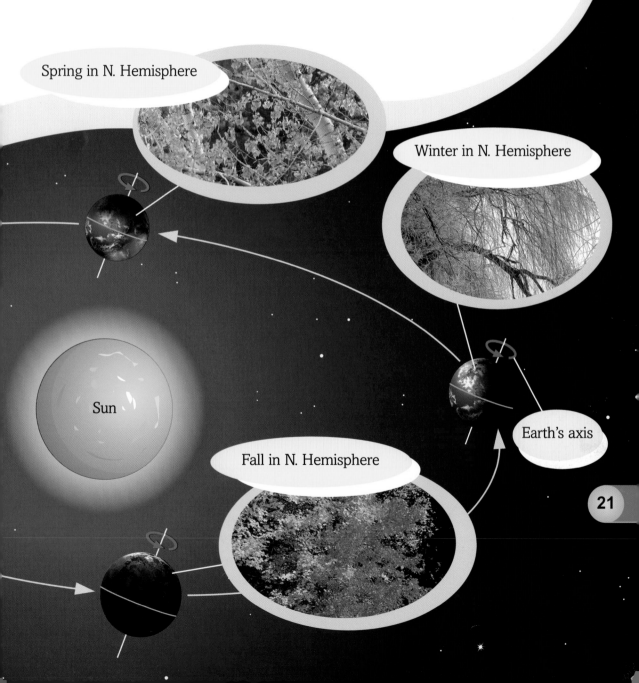

Spring in N. Hemisphere

Winter in N. Hemisphere

Sun

Fall in N. Hemisphere

Earth's axis

Endless summer and winter

Earth's **orbit** around the Sun causes the seasons: summer, winter, fall, and spring. If Earth stood still, the seasons would be stuck. So, if it was winter in the Northern **Hemisphere**, it would always be winter there.

When it is summer, the Sun's rays are stronger. There are more hours of daylight. It is warmer outside. In winter, the Sun's rays are more spread out. There are fewer hours of daylight. The land and sea heat up less. This makes it colder outside.

North Pole in darkness

sunlight

South Pole in daylight

The Midnight Sun

*Some people on Earth are used to long periods of daylight and darkness. Some places near the North and South **poles** have daylight for six months and darkness for six months! In the daylight months, the Sun can still be seen in the sky at midnight! This is called the midnight sun.*

▼ *If Earth stood still, some places would have endless winter.*

Many animals hibernate to save ▼ **energy**. The dormouse spends six months of the year asleep!

Patterns of living

Many animals behave differently in different seasons. Some birds spend summer and winter in different countries. They move to escape cold weather and to find food. They only lay their eggs in the spring.

Some animals **hibernate** in winter to escape the cold. This means they go into a long, deep sleep. In the spring, many baby animals are born. If we had no seasons, all of these important patterns of life would be destroyed.

Many plants have patterns of life that change with the seasons, too. Flowers bloom at different times of the year. Farmers plant their crops in the spring. They harvest the crops in the late summer.

If the seasons never changed, plants would not have the same growing patterns. Many plants would die. Animals that need plants for food would die, too.

hibernate   go into a long, deep sleep

The Real Danger

Of course, Earth will never stand still. The Sun's **gravity** keeps all the planets **orbiting** (circling) around it. However, there are some changes that could make life on Earth more dangerous.

The **ozone layer** is part of the **atmosphere**. It is high above Earth. It protects us from harmful rays from the Sun. These rays can cause sunburn and skin cancer. They can also damage our eyes. Life on Earth could not exist without the ozone layer.

Pollution caused by humans has made a hole in the ozone layer. Most air pollution happens when people burn oil, coal, or gas.

Pollution is also making the atmosphere warmer. This is called global warming. Many scientists think that global warming will change Earth's climate in the next 100 years.

atmosphere   layer of gases that surrounds Earth
ozone layer   part of the atmosphere high above Earth
pollution   something that poisons or damages air, water, or land

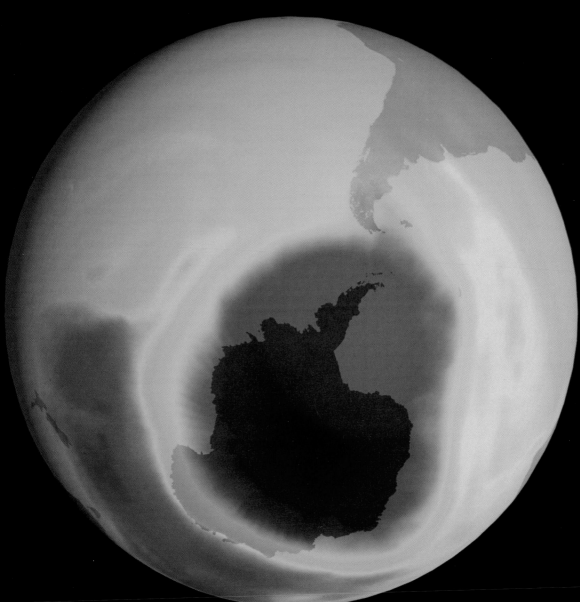

Round Up!

We have night and ▶
day because
Earth is spinning
on its axis.

Earth's axis

March 21

Spring begins in N. Hemisphere

Fall begins in S. Hemisphere

June 21

Summer begins in N. Hemisphere

Winter begins in S. Hemisphere

A giant leap!

Earth takes 365 days and six hours to **orbit** *the Sun. Yet a normal year only has 365 days. Every four years, we have a leap year. A leap year has 366 days. The extra day comes from adding together the extra six hours from each year.*

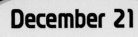

December 21

Winter begins in N. Hemisphere

Summer begins in S. Hemisphere

Sun

Earth's orbit

September 21

Fall begins in N. Hemisphere

Spring begins in S. Hemisphere

▲ *We have different seasons as Earth orbits the Sun. The seasons happen because Earth is tilted on its axis. This means that it is at different angles to the Sun at different times of the year.*

Glossary

atmosphere layer of gases that surrounds Earth. The ozone layer is part of Earth's atmosphere.

axis imaginary line passing through the center of Earth. Earth rotates around its axis.

energy ability to cause a change or make something move

equator imaginary line around the middle of Earth. The equator splits Earth into two halves.

food chain way animals are linked to other animals and to plants by what they eat

force something that acts to change the movement or shape of an object

friction force that slows two objects down if they are touching each other

gravity force that pulls large objects toward each other

hemisphere one half of Earth. The Northern Hemisphere is the top half of Earth. The Southern Hemisphere is the bottom half.

hibernate go into a long, deep sleep. Some animals hibernate in the winter to escape the cold.

hurricane tropical storm with very fast winds

magnetic field area around a magnetic object. The magnetic force of this area can affect other objects.

nocturnal most active at night. Animals such as owls and bats are nocturnal.

orbit move around something on a fixed path. Planets, such as Earth, orbit the Sun.

ozone layer part of the atmosphere high above Earth. The ozone layer protects us from harmful rays from the Sun.

phases stages. The phases of the Moon are the changing shapes of the Moon that we see as it orbits Earth.

photosynthesis how green plants make sugary food using light energy

pole one end of Earth's axis. There are two poles on Earth: the North Pole and the South Pole.

pollution something that poisons or damages air, water, or land. Air pollution can be caused by smoke.

rotate spin or turn on an axis. Earth takes 24 hours to rotate on its axis.

Want to Know More?

You can find out lots more about how Earth moves in space:

Books to read

• Clark, Stuart. *Earth*. Chicago: Heinemann Library, 2003.

• Cole, Michael D. *Earth: The Third Planet*. Berkeley Heights, N.J.: Enslow, 2001.

• Prinja, Raman K. *The Sun*. Chicago: Heinemann Library, 2003.

Websites

•http://www.nasa.gov/home/index.html

Would you like to learn more about space? Check out the students' section of the National Aeronautics and Space Administration (NASA) website to find out more about space and to play some games!

http://www.windows.ucar.edu/

Do you want to learn more about Earth and the other planets? Check out this website to learn more and to play some exciting games.

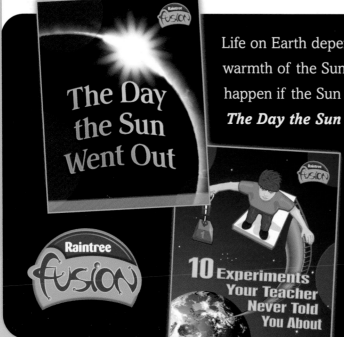

Life on Earth depends on the heat and warmth of the Sun. Find out what might happen if the Sun stopped shining in *The Day the Sun Went Out*.

Gravity keeps Earth in orbit around the Sun. Find out more about gravity in *10 Experiments Your Teacher Never Told You About*.

Index